50 Sex Tokens For Your Pleasure :)

This Belongs To:

_____

Eat my pussy really slow likes it's the best meal you've ever had and you never want it to end.

Good for a full body massage with a happy ending :)

Let me blindfold you and:

_____

_____

Learn how to give me
multiple orgasms...
Google is your friend :)

Plan an amazing date for us this week and when we get back fuck me the way you know i like it.

*Circle depending on your mood

Let's fuck/make love as we watch...

_____

Fuck me on/at/in

_____

*Circle as desired

Role Play

Me:

You:

Good for one
erotic movie of
my choice.

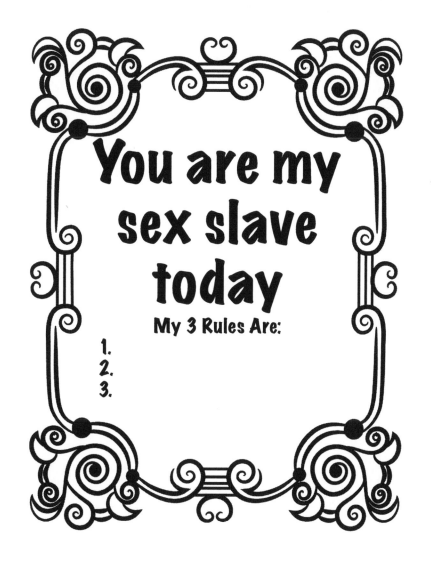

Good for sex
position of my
choice :)

Spank me ☐
I want to spank you ☐

*tick as desired

Blindfold me and:

_____

_____

_____

_____

Set up candles and wine.
Run a bath for me.
Bathe me gently and wash my hair.
Towel me down and then fuck me really slow and deep.
Afterwards hold me till i fall asleep.

Write me a
sexy letter
describing all
you want to
do for me...

No matter where we are or when, fuck me when i give you this.

Let's explore
Anal ...
but my rules
are:

_____

_____

_____

_____

_____

Fulfil my fantasy of

_____

_____

_____

_____

Dress up like a

_____

and seduce me slow/
fuck me fast

*Circle as desired

I want to
see you :

_____

_____

_____

_____

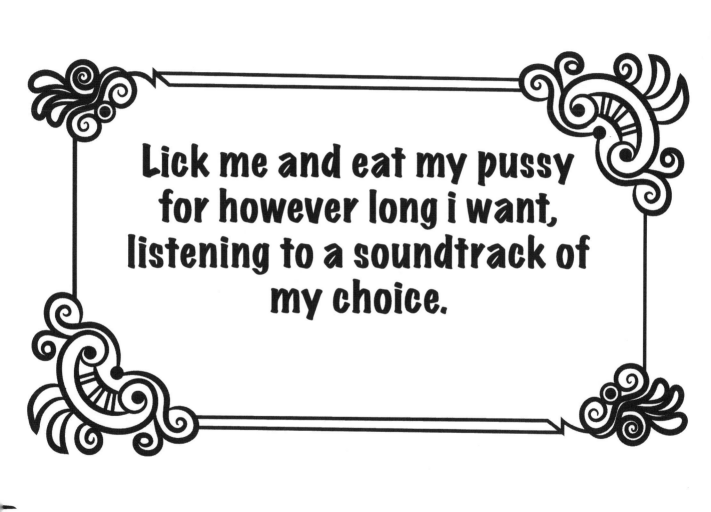

Do that one thing you know i like but you never want to do

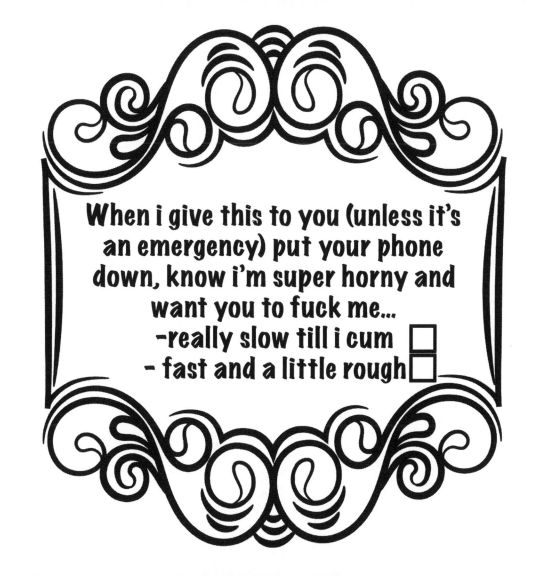

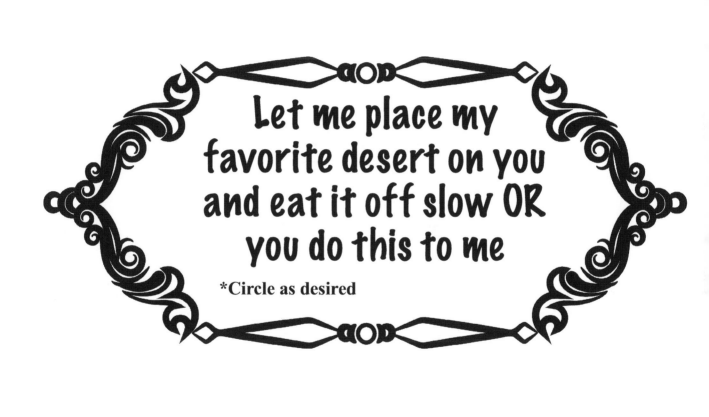

Let me place my favorite desert on you and eat it off slow OR you do this to me

*Circle as desired

Wear _____
for me and let's

I want you to:

_____

_____

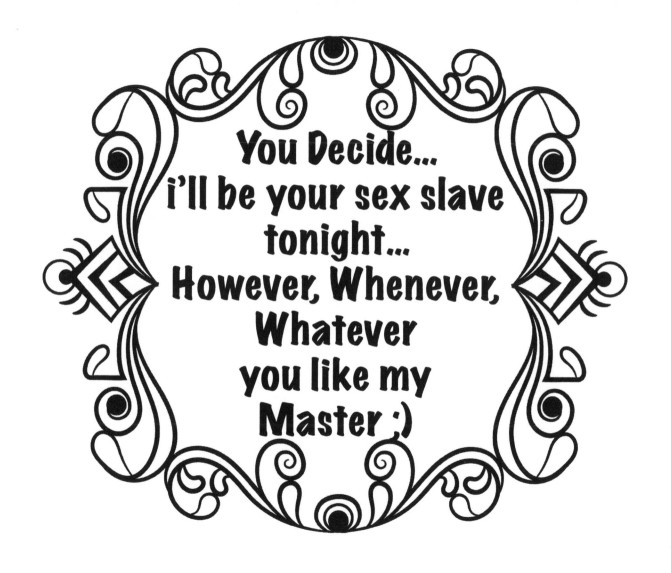

Sex Weekend Vacation or Staycation

*You & Me…Food, Drink and Sex The Way I Like All Weekend!

Made in the USA
San Bernardino, CA
27 July 2019